Sand, Leaf, or Coral Reef

A Book About Animal Habitats

by Patricia M. Stockland
illustrated by Todd Ouren

Special thanks to our advisers for their expertise:

Zoological Society of San Diego
San Diego Zoo
San Diego, California

Susan Kesselring, M.A., Literacy Educator
Rosemount-Apple Valley-Eagan (Minnesota) School District

PICTURE WINDOW BOOKS
Minneapolis, Minnesota

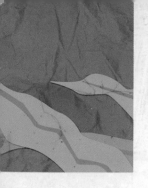

Managing Editor: Catherine Neitge
Creative Director: Terri Foley
Art Director: Keith Griffin
Editor: Christianne Jones
Designer: Todd Ouren
Page production: Picture Window Books
The illustrations in this book were prepared digitally.

Picture Window Books
5115 Excelsior Boulevard
Suite 232
Minneapolis, MN 55416
877-845-8392
www.picturewindowbooks.com

Printed in the United States of America.

Library of Congress Cataloging-in-Publication Data
Stockland, Patricia M.
Sand, leaf, or coral reef : a book about animal habitats/
by Patricia Stockland ; illustrated by Todd Ouren.
p. cm. — (Animal wise)
Includes bibliographical references (p.   ).
ISBN 1-4048-0932-5 (hardcover)
1. Habitat (Ecology)—Juvenile literature. I. Ouren, Todd, ill.
II. Title.

QH541.14.S76 2004
591.7—dc22   2004023307

Habitat Adaptations

Animals live almost everywhere, from the hottest desert to the coldest mountain. How do animals handle these different habitats?

They adapt to their surroundings. Some animals have protective fur that keeps them warm. Others have big noses to reach faraway food. Some animals even look like part of their home.

Discover how these animals live in so many different habitats.

River Otter

Sunlight sparkles on the water. The river otter splashes after a fish.

The otter is an expert fisherman. Its strong tail and webbed toes help it swim through the quick river currents. The animal's waterproof coat keeps the otter warm and dry.

The otter's tail is flat, wide, and long—just like a built-in paddle! It helps the otter swim down the river.

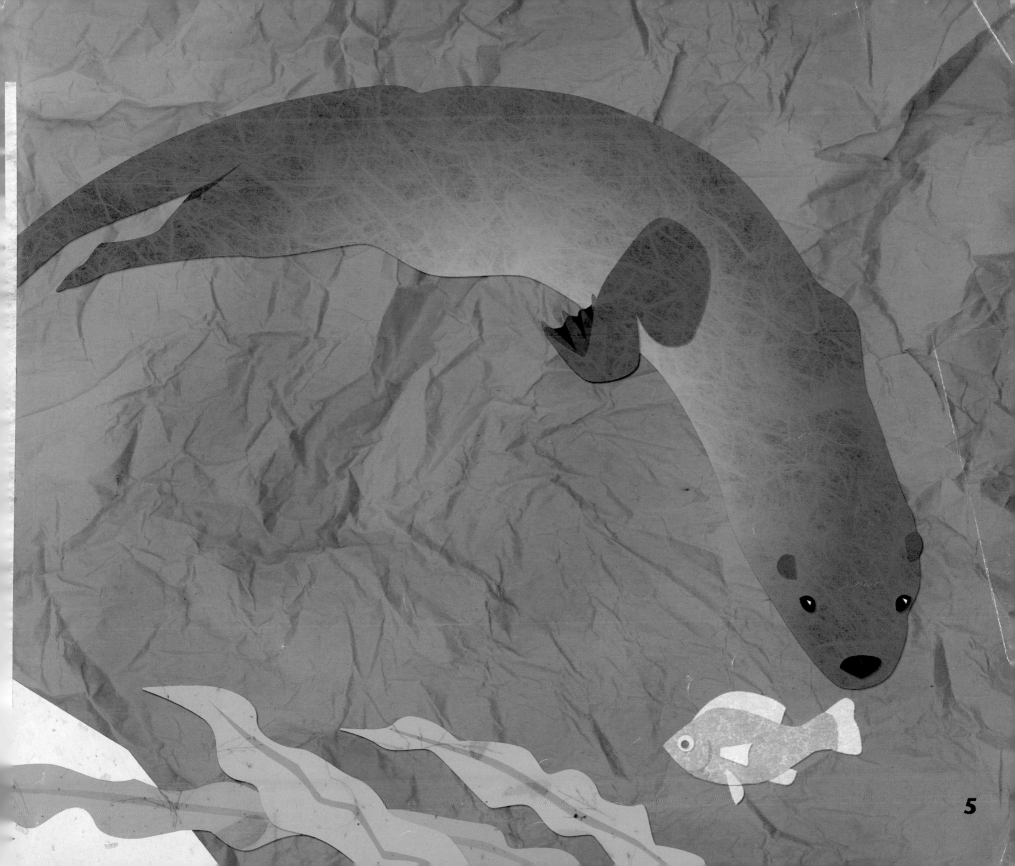

5

Clownfish

The bright coral reef bustles with life. A clownfish pokes its head out of the anemone to watch.

Plenty of predators would like to eat the clownfish. To be safe, the tiny fish stays near the stinging tentacles of the anemone. Slimy mucus covers the clownfish, which keeps it from getting stung.

If the clownfish leaves the anemone, it must quickly touch it again and again when it returns. After a while, the fish is safe from the stings. This is called building back immunity.

Alligator

The air is warm and wet in the marshy swamp. An alligator lurks in the muddy water.

The alligator's nostrils, ears, and eyes are on top of its head. This lets the animal hide partially under the water. The big reptile is still able to breathe and see approaching prey or predators.

Alligators have special skin flaps for diving into the swamp. These flaps close over the animal's nostrils, ears, and throat so water doesn't get in.

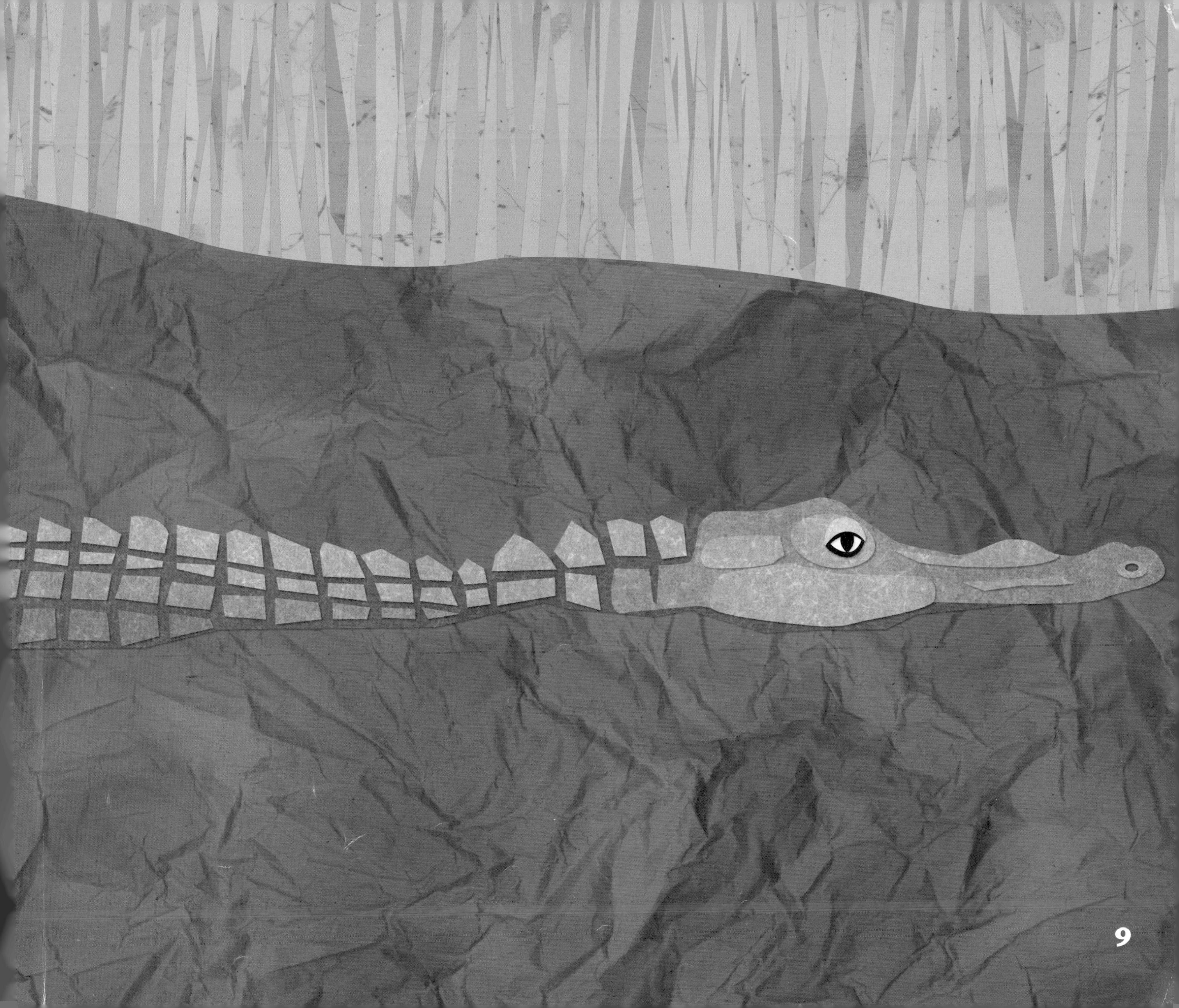

Snowy Owl

Snow covers the cold Arctic tundra. The snowy owl flies over the snow and ice looking for food.

White feathers help the owl sneak up on prey. The disguise also hides the bird from hungry predators. The snowy owl blends in with its snowy surroundings.

Female snowy owls have black markings, which help them blend in with their nests. Males are completely white to blend in with the snow.

Mountain Goat

Moss and grass grow along the snowline of the mountain. The mountain goat grazes on the steep slope.

Life on the mountainside can be dangerous and cold. The mountain goat stays warm with its shaggy coat. Its small, rough hooves let the animal quickly climb a wall of rock to escape any predators.

A mountain goat's hooves have rubberlike pads around the edges. These keep the animal from slipping on the mountainside.

Moose

Patches of sunlight fall on the forest floor. The mighty moose munches on twigs.

The moose is made for forest life. Its wide hooves and long legs help it walk through deep snow or deep water. And the moose's big mouth can grab large bites of tough food.

A moose has very flexible lips and a broad muzzle. These features help the animal strip leaves from small branches in the forest.

Giant Anteater

A termite mound hides in the tall, dry grass of the savanna. A giant anteater finds it.

Catching food in the savanna is no problem for the giant anteater. Its front feet have powerful claws that rip into a termite mound. The creature's long, sticky tongue sweeps around in the mound, gobbling up plenty of bugs.

A giant anteater also has a large, bushy tail. When the animal sleeps, it covers itself with this furry "blanket."

16

Toco Toucan

Hot, sticky air fills the tropical rain forest. The toucan lands on a fruit tree.

Ripe fruit hangs on tiny twigs. But the toucan is too big to perch on those fragile branches. Thanks to its long, bright bill, the bird can easily reach dinner on another branch.

A Toco toucan's bill can grow to be longer than a new pencil.

19

Camel

Wind blows across the dry desert. The camel walks slowly over hot, hot sand.

The camel is well suited for desert life. Long eyelashes protect its eyes from the blowing sand. Wide, furry feet keep the camel from sinking into the sand. A large hump stores fat. When food and water aren't available, the camel lives off the fat.

Camels help people survive desert life, too. The animals provide milk, hair, and transportation.

21

Do You Remember?

Point to the picture of the animal described in each question.

1. I live in the mountains, but the cold doesn't bother me.
   I run up the steep slopes with ease. Who am I?

   (mountain goat)

2. Having a big bill helps me in the hot rain forest. My perch
   may be far away, but I can still reach yummy fruit.
   Who am I?

   (Toco toucan)

3. I swim in the reef near my anemone friend. My mucus
   protects me from its stings. Who am I?

   (clownfish)

22

Fun Facts

Snowy owls protect themselves from the cold with lots of extra feathers. Their feathers cover most of their beak and their feet.

Alligators like to float. If their swamp or marsh starts to dry up, the reptiles will go into "alligator holes." These are small, muddy bodies of water that the alligator keeps digging out.

In the winter, moose shed their enormous antlers. In the spring, the antlers grow back even bigger than the year before.

The toucan's bright colors help it find other toucans in the thick, tropical forest.

The relationship between the anemone and the clownfish is symbiotic. That means they help each other. The anemone offers protection to the clownfish. In return, the clownfish keeps the anemone clean by eating its leftovers

Glossary

disguise—changing the way something looks in order to hide it or not show what it really is

habitat— a place where plants and animals live

immunity—an ability to resist things such as sickness or stings

mucus—a slimy liquid that usually protects a body part

predator—an animal that hunts and eats other animals

prey—an animal that is hunted by another animal for food

savanna—a grassy plain with only a few trees

surroundings—the area around something, such as its habitat or environment

tentacles—long, flexible limbs (like legs or arms), used for moving, feeling, and grabbing

TO LEARN MORE

At the Library

Dahl, Michael. *Do Ducks Live in the Desert? A Book About Where Animals Live.* Minneapolis: Picture Window Books, 2004.

Fitzsimons, Cecilia. *Animal Habitats.* Austin, Tex.: Raintree Steck-Vaughn, 1996.

Ganeri, Anita. *Animal Homes.* Philadelphia: Chelsea House Publishers, 2004.

On the Web

FactHound offers a safe, fun way to find Web sites related to this book. All of the sites on FactHound have been researched by our staff. *www.facthound.com*

1. Visit the FactHound home page.
2. Enter a search word related to this book, or type in this special code: 1404809325
3. Click the FETCH IT button.

Your trusty FactHound will fetch the best Web sites for you!

INDEX

Look for all of the books in the Animal Wise series:

Pointy, Long, or Round
A Book About Animal Shapes

Sand, Leaf, or Coral Reef
A Book About Animal Habitats

Stripes, Spots, or Diamonds
A Book About Animal Patterns

Red Eyes or Blue Feathers
A Book About Animal Colors

Strange Dances and Long Flights
A Book About Animal Behavior

Swing, Slither, or Swim
A Book About Animal Movements